THIS BUCKET LIST BELONGS TO

. . . .

COPYRIGHT © PROTECTED BY HANNAH O'HARRIET

All rights reserved. No part of this publication may be reproduced, distributed, or transmitted in any form or by any means, including photocopying, recording, or other electronic or mechanical methods, without prior written permission of the author, except in the case of brief quotations embodied in critical reviews and certain other non-commercial uses permitted by copyright law.

THE BUCKETLIST

1. .... ☐
2. .... ☐
3. .... ☐
4. .... ☐
5. .... ☐
6. .... ☐
7. .... ☐
8. .... ☐
9. .... ☐
10. .... ☐
11. .... ☐
12. .... ☐
13. .... ☐
14. .... ☐
15. .... ☐
16. .... ☐
17. .... ☐
18. .... ☐
19. .... ☐
20. .... ☐

THE BUCKETLIST

21. .... ☐
22. .... ☐
23. .... ☐
24. .... ☐
25. .... ☐
26. .... ☐
27. .... ☐
28. .... ☐
29. .... ☐
30. .... ☐
31. .... ☐
32. .... ☐
33. .... ☐
34. .... ☐
35. .... ☐
36. .... ☐
37. .... ☐
38. .... ☐
39. .... ☐
40. .... ☐

THE
BUCKETLIST

41 .... ☐
42 .... ☐
43 .... ☐
44 .... ☐
45 .... ☐
46 .... ☐
47 .... ☐
48 .... ☐
49 .... ☐
50 .... ☐
51 .... ☐
52 .... ☐
53 .... ☐
54 .... ☐
55 .... ☐
56 .... ☐
57 .... ☐
58 .... ☐
59 .... ☐
60 .... ☐

THE BUCKETLIST

61 .... ☐
62 .... ☐
63 .... ☐
64 .... ☐
65 .... ☐
66 .... ☐
67 .... ☐
68 .... ☐
69 .... ☐
70 .... ☐
71 .... ☐
72 .... ☐
73 .... ☐
74 .... ☐
75 .... ☐
76 .... ☐
77 .... ☐
78 .... ☐
79 .... ☐
80 .... ☐

THE BUCKETLIST

81 .... ☐
82 .... ☐
83 .... ☐
84 .... ☐
85 .... ☐
86 .... ☐
87 .... ☐
88 .... ☐
89 .... ☐
90 .... ☐
91 .... ☐
92 .... ☐
93 .... ☐
94 .... ☐
95 .... ☐
96 .... ☐
97 .... ☐
98 .... ☐
99 .... ☐
100 .... ☐

1

I WANT TO DO THIS BECAUSE ....

....

TO MAKE THIS HAPPEN I NEED ....

....

DATE COMPLETED ....

WHERE ....

SOLO – WITH ....

THE STORY

....

....

THE BEST PART

....

....

WHAT I LEARNED FROM THIS

....

....

WOULD I DO IT AGAIN? ....

2

I WANT TO DO THIS BECAUSE

TO MAKE THIS HAPPEN I NEED

DATE COMPLETED

WHERE

SOLO – WITH

THE STORY

THE BEST PART

WHAT I LEARNED FROM THIS

WOULD I DO IT AGAIN?

I WANT TO DO THIS BECAUSE

....

TO MAKE THIS HAPPEN I NEED

....

DATE COMPLETED ....

WHERE ....

SOLO – WITH ....

THE STORY

....

....

THE BEST PART

....

....

WHAT I LEARNED FROM THIS

....

....

WOULD I DO IT AGAIN? ....

4

I WANT TO DO THIS BECAUSE

TO MAKE THIS HAPPEN I NEED

DATE COMPLETED

WHERE

SOLO – WITH

THE STORY

THE BEST PART

WHAT I LEARNED FROM THIS

WOULD I DO IT AGAIN?

5

I WANT TO DO THIS BECAUSE

TO MAKE THIS HAPPEN I NEED

DATE COMPLETED

WHERE

SOLO – WITH

THE STORY

THE BEST PART

WHAT I LEARNED FROM THIS

WOULD I DO IT AGAIN?

I WANT TO DO THIS BECAUSE

TO MAKE THIS HAPPEN I NEED

DATE COMPLETED

WHERE

SOLO – WITH

THE STORY

THE BEST PART

WHAT I LEARNED FROM THIS

WOULD I DO IT AGAIN?

7

I WANT TO DO THIS BECAUSE

TO MAKE THIS HAPPEN I NEED

DATE COMPLETED

WHERE

SOLO – WITH

THE STORY

THE BEST PART

WHAT I LEARNED FROM THIS

WOULD I DO IT AGAIN?

I WANT TO DO THIS BECAUSE

TO MAKE THIS HAPPEN I NEED

DATE COMPLETED

WHERE

SOLO – WITH

THE STORY

THE BEST PART

WHAT I LEARNED FROM THIS

WOULD I DO IT AGAIN?

I WANT TO DO THIS BECAUSE

TO MAKE THIS HAPPEN I NEED

DATE COMPLETED

WHERE

SOLO – WITH

THE STORY

THE BEST PART

WHAT I LEARNED FROM THIS

WOULD I DO IT AGAIN?

10

I WANT TO DO THIS BECAUSE

TO MAKE THIS HAPPEN I NEED

DATE COMPLETED

WHERE

SOLO – WITH

THE STORY

THE BEST PART

WHAT I LEARNED FROM THIS

WOULD I DO IT AGAIN?

11

I WANT TO DO THIS BECAUSE

TO MAKE THIS HAPPEN I NEED

DATE COMPLETED

WHERE

SOLO – WITH

THE STORY

THE BEST PART

WHAT I LEARNED FROM THIS

WOULD I DO IT AGAIN?

12

I WANT TO DO THIS BECAUSE

TO MAKE THIS HAPPEN I NEED

DATE COMPLETED

WHERE

SOLO – WITH

THE STORY

THE BEST PART

WHAT I LEARNED FROM THIS

WOULD I DO IT AGAIN?

13

I WANT TO DO THIS BECAUSE ....

TO MAKE THIS HAPPEN I NEED ....

DATE COMPLETED ....

WHERE ....

SOLO – WITH ....

THE STORY

....

....

THE BEST PART

....

....

WHAT I LEARNED FROM THIS

....

....

WOULD I DO IT AGAIN? ....

14

I WANT TO DO THIS BECAUSE

TO MAKE THIS HAPPEN I NEED

DATE COMPLETED

WHERE

SOLO – WITH

THE STORY

THE BEST PART

WHAT I LEARNED FROM THIS

WOULD I DO IT AGAIN?

15

I WANT TO DO THIS BECAUSE

TO MAKE THIS HAPPEN I NEED

DATE COMPLETED

WHERE

SOLO – WITH

THE STORY

THE BEST PART

WHAT I LEARNED FROM THIS

WOULD I DO IT AGAIN?

16

I WANT TO DO THIS BECAUSE

....

....

TO MAKE THIS HAPPEN I NEED

....

DATE COMPLETED ....

WHERE ....

SOLO – WITH ....

THE STORY

....

....

THE BEST PART

....

....

WHAT I LEARNED FROM THIS

....

....

WOULD I DO IT AGAIN? ....

17

I WANT TO DO THIS BECAUSE

TO MAKE THIS HAPPEN I NEED

DATE COMPLETED

WHERE

SOLO – WITH

THE STORY

THE BEST PART

WHAT I LEARNED FROM THIS

WOULD I DO IT AGAIN?

18

I WANT TO DO THIS BECAUSE

TO MAKE THIS HAPPEN I NEED

DATE COMPLETED

WHERE

SOLO – WITH

THE STORY

THE BEST PART

WHAT I LEARNED FROM THIS

WOULD I DO IT AGAIN?

19

I WANT TO DO THIS BECAUSE

TO MAKE THIS HAPPEN I NEED

DATE COMPLETED

WHERE

SOLO – WITH

THE STORY

THE BEST PART

WHAT I LEARNED FROM THIS

WOULD I DO IT AGAIN?

20

I WANT TO DO THIS BECAUSE

TO MAKE THIS HAPPEN I NEED

DATE COMPLETED

WHERE

SOLO – WITH

THE STORY

THE BEST PART

WHAT I LEARNED FROM THIS

WOULD I DO IT AGAIN?

21

I WANT TO DO THIS BECAUSE

TO MAKE THIS HAPPEN I NEED

DATE COMPLETED

WHERE

SOLO – WITH

THE STORY

THE BEST PART

WHAT I LEARNED FROM THIS

WOULD I DO IT AGAIN?

22

I WANT TO DO THIS BECAUSE

TO MAKE THIS HAPPEN I NEED

DATE COMPLETED

WHERE

SOLO – WITH

THE STORY

THE BEST PART

WHAT I LEARNED FROM THIS

WOULD I DO IT AGAIN?

23

I WANT TO DO THIS BECAUSE

TO MAKE THIS HAPPEN I NEED

DATE COMPLETED

WHERE

SOLO – WITH

THE STORY

THE BEST PART

WHAT I LEARNED FROM THIS

WOULD I DO IT AGAIN?

24

I WANT TO DO THIS BECAUSE

TO MAKE THIS HAPPEN I NEED

DATE COMPLETED

WHERE

SOLO – WITH

THE STORY

THE BEST PART

WHAT I LEARNED FROM THIS

WOULD I DO IT AGAIN?

25

I WANT TO DO THIS BECAUSE
....

TO MAKE THIS HAPPEN I NEED
....

DATE COMPLETED ....

WHERE ....

SOLO – WITH ....

THE STORY
....
....

THE BEST PART
....
....

WHAT I LEARNED FROM THIS
....
....

WOULD I DO IT AGAIN? ....

26

I WANT TO DO THIS BECAUSE

TO MAKE THIS HAPPEN I NEED

DATE COMPLETED

WHERE

SOLO – WITH

THE STORY

THE BEST PART

WHAT I LEARNED FROM THIS

WOULD I DO IT AGAIN?

27

I WANT TO DO THIS BECAUSE

TO MAKE THIS HAPPEN I NEED

DATE COMPLETED

WHERE

SOLO – WITH

THE STORY

THE BEST PART

WHAT I LEARNED FROM THIS

WOULD I DO IT AGAIN?

28

I WANT TO DO THIS BECAUSE

TO MAKE THIS HAPPEN I NEED

DATE COMPLETED

WHERE

SOLO – WITH

THE STORY

THE BEST PART

WHAT I LEARNED FROM THIS

WOULD I DO IT AGAIN?

29

I WANT TO DO THIS BECAUSE

TO MAKE THIS HAPPEN I NEED

DATE COMPLETED

WHERE

SOLO – WITH

THE STORY

THE BEST PART

WHAT I LEARNED FROM THIS

WOULD I DO IT AGAIN?

30

I WANT TO DO THIS BECAUSE
....

....

TO MAKE THIS HAPPEN I NEED
....

DATE COMPLETED ....

WHERE ....

SOLO – WITH ....

THE STORY
....

....

THE BEST PART
....

....

WHAT I LEARNED FROM THIS
....

....

WOULD I DO IT AGAIN? ....

31

I WANT TO DO THIS BECAUSE

TO MAKE THIS HAPPEN I NEED

DATE COMPLETED

WHERE

SOLO – WITH

THE STORY

THE BEST PART

WHAT I LEARNED FROM THIS

WOULD I DO IT AGAIN?

32

I WANT TO DO THIS BECAUSE

TO MAKE THIS HAPPEN I NEED

DATE COMPLETED

WHERE

SOLO – WITH

THE STORY

THE BEST PART

WHAT I LEARNED FROM THIS

WOULD I DO IT AGAIN?

33

I WANT TO DO THIS BECAUSE

TO MAKE THIS HAPPEN I NEED

DATE COMPLETED

WHERE

SOLO – WITH

THE STORY

THE BEST PART

WHAT I LEARNED FROM THIS

WOULD I DO IT AGAIN?

34

I WANT TO DO THIS BECAUSE

TO MAKE THIS HAPPEN I NEED

DATE COMPLETED

WHERE

SOLO – WITH

THE STORY

THE BEST PART

WHAT I LEARNED FROM THIS

WOULD I DO IT AGAIN?

35

I WANT TO DO THIS BECAUSE

TO MAKE THIS HAPPEN I NEED

DATE COMPLETED

WHERE

SOLO – WITH

THE STORY

THE BEST PART

WHAT I LEARNED FROM THIS

WOULD I DO IT AGAIN?

36

I WANT TO DO THIS BECAUSE

TO MAKE THIS HAPPEN I NEED

DATE COMPLETED

WHERE

SOLO – WITH

THE STORY

THE BEST PART

WHAT I LEARNED FROM THIS

WOULD I DO IT AGAIN?

37

I WANT TO DO THIS BECAUSE

TO MAKE THIS HAPPEN I NEED

DATE COMPLETED

WHERE

SOLO – WITH

THE STORY

THE BEST PART

WHAT I LEARNED FROM THIS

WOULD I DO IT AGAIN?

38

I WANT TO DO THIS BECAUSE

TO MAKE THIS HAPPEN I NEED

DATE COMPLETED

WHERE

SOLO – WITH

THE STORY

THE BEST PART

WHAT I LEARNED FROM THIS

WOULD I DO IT AGAIN?

39

I WANT TO DO THIS BECAUSE

TO MAKE THIS HAPPEN I NEED

DATE COMPLETED

WHERE

SOLO – WITH

THE STORY

THE BEST PART

WHAT I LEARNED FROM THIS

WOULD I DO IT AGAIN?

40

I WANT TO DO THIS BECAUSE

TO MAKE THIS HAPPEN I NEED

DATE COMPLETED

WHERE

SOLO – WITH

THE STORY

THE BEST PART

WHAT I LEARNED FROM THIS

WOULD I DO IT AGAIN?

41

I WANT TO DO THIS BECAUSE

TO MAKE THIS HAPPEN I NEED

DATE COMPLETED

WHERE

SOLO – WITH

THE STORY

THE BEST PART

WHAT I LEARNED FROM THIS

WOULD I DO IT AGAIN?

42

I WANT TO DO THIS BECAUSE

TO MAKE THIS HAPPEN I NEED

DATE COMPLETED

WHERE

SOLO – WITH

THE STORY

THE BEST PART

WHAT I LEARNED FROM THIS

WOULD I DO IT AGAIN?

43

I WANT TO DO THIS BECAUSE

TO MAKE THIS HAPPEN I NEED

DATE COMPLETED

WHERE

SOLO – WITH

THE STORY

THE BEST PART

WHAT I LEARNED FROM THIS

WOULD I DO IT AGAIN?

44

I WANT TO DO THIS BECAUSE

TO MAKE THIS HAPPEN I NEED

DATE COMPLETED

WHERE

SOLO – WITH

THE STORY

THE BEST PART

WHAT I LEARNED FROM THIS

WOULD I DO IT AGAIN?

45

I WANT TO DO THIS BECAUSE

TO MAKE THIS HAPPEN I NEED

DATE COMPLETED

WHERE

SOLO – WITH

THE STORY

THE BEST PART

WHAT I LEARNED FROM THIS

WOULD I DO IT AGAIN?

46

I WANT TO DO THIS BECAUSE

TO MAKE THIS HAPPEN I NEED

DATE COMPLETED

WHERE

SOLO – WITH

THE STORY

THE BEST PART

WHAT I LEARNED FROM THIS

WOULD I DO IT AGAIN?

47

I WANT TO DO THIS BECAUSE

TO MAKE THIS HAPPEN I NEED

DATE COMPLETED

WHERE

SOLO – WITH

THE STORY

THE BEST PART

WHAT I LEARNED FROM THIS

WOULD I DO IT AGAIN?

48

I WANT TO DO THIS BECAUSE

TO MAKE THIS HAPPEN I NEED

DATE COMPLETED

WHERE

SOLO – WITH

THE STORY

THE BEST PART

WHAT I LEARNED FROM THIS

WOULD I DO IT AGAIN?

49

I WANT TO DO THIS BECAUSE

TO MAKE THIS HAPPEN I NEED

DATE COMPLETED

WHERE

SOLO – WITH

THE STORY

THE BEST PART

WHAT I LEARNED FROM THIS

WOULD I DO IT AGAIN?

50

I WANT TO DO THIS BECAUSE

TO MAKE THIS HAPPEN I NEED

DATE COMPLETED

WHERE

SOLO – WITH

THE STORY

THE BEST PART

WHAT I LEARNED FROM THIS

WOULD I DO IT AGAIN?

51

I WANT TO DO THIS BECAUSE

TO MAKE THIS HAPPEN I NEED

DATE COMPLETED

WHERE

SOLO – WITH

THE STORY

THE BEST PART

WHAT I LEARNED FROM THIS

WOULD I DO IT AGAIN?

52

I WANT TO DO THIS BECAUSE

TO MAKE THIS HAPPEN I NEED

DATE COMPLETED

WHERE

SOLO – WITH

THE STORY

THE BEST PART

WHAT I LEARNED FROM THIS

WOULD I DO IT AGAIN?

53

I WANT TO DO THIS BECAUSE

TO MAKE THIS HAPPEN I NEED

DATE COMPLETED

WHERE

SOLO – WITH

THE STORY

THE BEST PART

WHAT I LEARNED FROM THIS

WOULD I DO IT AGAIN?

54

I WANT TO DO THIS BECAUSE

TO MAKE THIS HAPPEN I NEED

DATE COMPLETED

WHERE

SOLO – WITH

THE STORY

THE BEST PART

WHAT I LEARNED FROM THIS

WOULD I DO IT AGAIN?

55

I WANT TO DO THIS BECAUSE

....

TO MAKE THIS HAPPEN I NEED

....

DATE COMPLETED ....

WHERE ....

SOLO – WITH ....

THE STORY

....

....

THE BEST PART

....

....

WHAT I LEARNED FROM THIS

....

....

WOULD I DO IT AGAIN? ....

56

I WANT TO DO THIS BECAUSE

TO MAKE THIS HAPPEN I NEED

DATE COMPLETED

WHERE

SOLO – WITH

THE STORY

THE BEST PART

WHAT I LEARNED FROM THIS

WOULD I DO IT AGAIN?

57

I WANT TO DO THIS BECAUSE

TO MAKE THIS HAPPEN I NEED

DATE COMPLETED

WHERE

SOLO – WITH

THE STORY

THE BEST PART

WHAT I LEARNED FROM THIS

WOULD I DO IT AGAIN?

58

I WANT TO DO THIS BECAUSE

TO MAKE THIS HAPPEN I NEED

DATE COMPLETED

WHERE

SOLO – WITH

THE STORY

THE BEST PART

WHAT I LEARNED FROM THIS

WOULD I DO IT AGAIN?

59

I WANT TO DO THIS BECAUSE

TO MAKE THIS HAPPEN I NEED

DATE COMPLETED

WHERE

SOLO – WITH

THE STORY

THE BEST PART

WHAT I LEARNED FROM THIS

WOULD I DO IT AGAIN?

60

I WANT TO DO THIS BECAUSE

TO MAKE THIS HAPPEN I NEED

DATE COMPLETED

WHERE

SOLO – WITH

THE STORY

THE BEST PART

WHAT I LEARNED FROM THIS

WOULD I DO IT AGAIN?

61

I WANT TO DO THIS BECAUSE

TO MAKE THIS HAPPEN I NEED

DATE COMPLETED

WHERE

SOLO – WITH

THE STORY

THE BEST PART

WHAT I LEARNED FROM THIS

WOULD I DO IT AGAIN?

62

I WANT TO DO THIS BECAUSE

TO MAKE THIS HAPPEN I NEED

DATE COMPLETED

WHERE

SOLO – WITH

THE STORY

THE BEST PART

WHAT I LEARNED FROM THIS

WOULD I DO IT AGAIN?

63

I WANT TO DO THIS BECAUSE

TO MAKE THIS HAPPEN I NEED

DATE COMPLETED

WHERE

SOLO – WITH

THE STORY

THE BEST PART

WHAT I LEARNED FROM THIS

WOULD I DO IT AGAIN?

64

I WANT TO DO THIS BECAUSE

TO MAKE THIS HAPPEN I NEED

DATE COMPLETED

WHERE

SOLO – WITH

THE STORY

THE BEST PART

WHAT I LEARNED FROM THIS

WOULD I DO IT AGAIN?

65

I WANT TO DO THIS BECAUSE

TO MAKE THIS HAPPEN I NEED

DATE COMPLETED

WHERE

SOLO – WITH

THE STORY

THE BEST PART

WHAT I LEARNED FROM THIS

WOULD I DO IT AGAIN?

66

I WANT TO DO THIS BECAUSE

TO MAKE THIS HAPPEN I NEED

DATE COMPLETED

WHERE

SOLO – WITH

THE STORY

THE BEST PART

WHAT I LEARNED FROM THIS

WOULD I DO IT AGAIN?

67

I WANT TO DO THIS BECAUSE

TO MAKE THIS HAPPEN I NEED

DATE COMPLETED

WHERE

SOLO – WITH

THE STORY

THE BEST PART

WHAT I LEARNED FROM THIS

WOULD I DO IT AGAIN?

68

I WANT TO DO THIS BECAUSE

TO MAKE THIS HAPPEN I NEED

DATE COMPLETED

WHERE

SOLO – WITH

THE STORY

THE BEST PART

WHAT I LEARNED FROM THIS

WOULD I DO IT AGAIN?

69

I WANT TO DO THIS BECAUSE

TO MAKE THIS HAPPEN I NEED

DATE COMPLETED

WHERE

SOLO – WITH

THE STORY

THE BEST PART

WHAT I LEARNED FROM THIS

WOULD I DO IT AGAIN?

70

I WANT TO DO THIS BECAUSE

TO MAKE THIS HAPPEN I NEED

DATE COMPLETED

WHERE

SOLO – WITH

THE STORY

THE BEST PART

WHAT I LEARNED FROM THIS

WOULD I DO IT AGAIN?

71

I WANT TO DO THIS BECAUSE

TO MAKE THIS HAPPEN I NEED

DATE COMPLETED

WHERE

SOLO – WITH

THE STORY

THE BEST PART

WHAT I LEARNED FROM THIS

WOULD I DO IT AGAIN?

72

I WANT TO DO THIS BECAUSE

TO MAKE THIS HAPPEN I NEED

DATE COMPLETED

WHERE

SOLO – WITH

THE STORY

THE BEST PART

WHAT I LEARNED FROM THIS

WOULD I DO IT AGAIN?

73

I WANT TO DO THIS BECAUSE

TO MAKE THIS HAPPEN I NEED

DATE COMPLETED

WHERE

SOLO – WITH

THE STORY

THE BEST PART

WHAT I LEARNED FROM THIS

WOULD I DO IT AGAIN?

74

I WANT TO DO THIS BECAUSE

TO MAKE THIS HAPPEN I NEED

DATE COMPLETED

WHERE

SOLO – WITH

THE STORY

THE BEST PART

WHAT I LEARNED FROM THIS

WOULD I DO IT AGAIN?

75

I WANT TO DO THIS BECAUSE

TO MAKE THIS HAPPEN I NEED

DATE COMPLETED

WHERE

SOLO – WITH

THE STORY

THE BEST PART

WHAT I LEARNED FROM THIS

WOULD I DO IT AGAIN?

76

I WANT TO DO THIS BECAUSE

TO MAKE THIS HAPPEN I NEED

DATE COMPLETED

WHERE

SOLO – WITH

THE STORY

THE BEST PART

WHAT I LEARNED FROM THIS

WOULD I DO IT AGAIN?

77

I WANT TO DO THIS BECAUSE

TO MAKE THIS HAPPEN I NEED

DATE COMPLETED

WHERE

SOLO – WITH

THE STORY

THE BEST PART

WHAT I LEARNED FROM THIS

WOULD I DO IT AGAIN?

78

I WANT TO DO THIS BECAUSE

TO MAKE THIS HAPPEN I NEED

DATE COMPLETED

WHERE

SOLO – WITH

THE STORY

THE BEST PART

WHAT I LEARNED FROM THIS

WOULD I DO IT AGAIN?

79

I WANT TO DO THIS BECAUSE

TO MAKE THIS HAPPEN I NEED

DATE COMPLETED

WHERE

SOLO – WITH

THE STORY

THE BEST PART

WHAT I LEARNED FROM THIS

WOULD I DO IT AGAIN?

I WANT TO DO THIS BECAUSE

TO MAKE THIS HAPPEN I NEED

DATE COMPLETED

WHERE

SOLO – WITH

THE STORY

THE BEST PART

WHAT I LEARNED FROM THIS

WOULD I DO IT AGAIN?

81

I WANT TO DO THIS BECAUSE

TO MAKE THIS HAPPEN I NEED

DATE COMPLETED

WHERE

SOLO – WITH

THE STORY

THE BEST PART

WHAT I LEARNED FROM THIS

WOULD I DO IT AGAIN?

82

I WANT TO DO THIS BECAUSE

TO MAKE THIS HAPPEN I NEED

DATE COMPLETED

WHERE

SOLO – WITH

THE STORY

THE BEST PART

WHAT I LEARNED FROM THIS

WOULD I DO IT AGAIN?

83

I WANT TO DO THIS BECAUSE

TO MAKE THIS HAPPEN I NEED

DATE COMPLETED

WHERE

SOLO – WITH

THE STORY

THE BEST PART

WHAT I LEARNED FROM THIS

WOULD I DO IT AGAIN?

84

I WANT TO DO THIS BECAUSE

TO MAKE THIS HAPPEN I NEED

DATE COMPLETED

WHERE

SOLO – WITH

THE STORY

THE BEST PART

WHAT I LEARNED FROM THIS

WOULD I DO IT AGAIN?

85

I WANT TO DO THIS BECAUSE

TO MAKE THIS HAPPEN I NEED

DATE COMPLETED

WHERE

SOLO – WITH

THE STORY

THE BEST PART

WHAT I LEARNED FROM THIS

WOULD I DO IT AGAIN?

86

I WANT TO DO THIS BECAUSE

TO MAKE THIS HAPPEN I NEED

DATE COMPLETED

WHERE

SOLO – WITH

THE STORY

THE BEST PART

WHAT I LEARNED FROM THIS

WOULD I DO IT AGAIN?

87

I WANT TO DO THIS BECAUSE

TO MAKE THIS HAPPEN I NEED

DATE COMPLETED

WHERE

SOLO – WITH

THE STORY

THE BEST PART

WHAT I LEARNED FROM THIS

WOULD I DO IT AGAIN?

88

I WANT TO DO THIS BECAUSE

TO MAKE THIS HAPPEN I NEED

DATE COMPLETED

WHERE

SOLO – WITH

THE STORY

THE BEST PART

WHAT I LEARNED FROM THIS

WOULD I DO IT AGAIN?

89

I WANT TO DO THIS BECAUSE

TO MAKE THIS HAPPEN I NEED

DATE COMPLETED

WHERE

SOLO – WITH

THE STORY

THE BEST PART

WHAT I LEARNED FROM THIS

WOULD I DO IT AGAIN?

I WANT TO DO THIS BECAUSE

TO MAKE THIS HAPPEN I NEED

DATE COMPLETED

WHERE

SOLO – WITH

THE STORY

THE BEST PART

WHAT I LEARNED FROM THIS

WOULD I DO IT AGAIN?

91

I WANT TO DO THIS BECAUSE

TO MAKE THIS HAPPEN I NEED

DATE COMPLETED

WHERE

SOLO – WITH

THE STORY

THE BEST PART

WHAT I LEARNED FROM THIS

WOULD I DO IT AGAIN?

92

I WANT TO DO THIS BECAUSE

TO MAKE THIS HAPPEN I NEED

DATE COMPLETED

WHERE

SOLO – WITH

THE STORY

THE BEST PART

WHAT I LEARNED FROM THIS

WOULD I DO IT AGAIN?

93

I WANT TO DO THIS BECAUSE

TO MAKE THIS HAPPEN I NEED

DATE COMPLETED

WHERE

SOLO – WITH

THE STORY

THE BEST PART

WHAT I LEARNED FROM THIS

WOULD I DO IT AGAIN?

94

I WANT TO DO THIS BECAUSE

TO MAKE THIS HAPPEN I NEED

DATE COMPLETED

WHERE

SOLO – WITH

THE STORY

THE BEST PART

WHAT I LEARNED FROM THIS

WOULD I DO IT AGAIN?

95

I WANT TO DO THIS BECAUSE

TO MAKE THIS HAPPEN I NEED

DATE COMPLETED

WHERE

SOLO – WITH

THE STORY

THE BEST PART

WHAT I LEARNED FROM THIS

WOULD I DO IT AGAIN?

96

I WANT TO DO THIS BECAUSE

TO MAKE THIS HAPPEN I NEED

DATE COMPLETED

WHERE

SOLO – WITH

THE STORY

THE BEST PART

WHAT I LEARNED FROM THIS

WOULD I DO IT AGAIN?

97

I WANT TO DO THIS BECAUSE

....

TO MAKE THIS HAPPEN I NEED

....

DATE COMPLETED ....

WHERE ....

SOLO – WITH ....

THE STORY

....

....

THE BEST PART

....

....

WHAT I LEARNED FROM THIS

....

....

WOULD I DO IT AGAIN? ....

98

I WANT TO DO THIS BECAUSE

TO MAKE THIS HAPPEN I NEED

DATE COMPLETED

WHERE

SOLO – WITH

THE STORY

THE BEST PART

WHAT I LEARNED FROM THIS

WOULD I DO IT AGAIN?

99

I WANT TO DO THIS BECAUSE
....

....

TO MAKE THIS HAPPEN I NEED
....

DATE COMPLETED ....

WHERE ....

SOLO – WITH ....

THE STORY
....

....

THE BEST PART
....

....

WHAT I LEARNED FROM THIS
....

....

WOULD I DO IT AGAIN? ....

100

I WANT TO DO THIS BECAUSE

TO MAKE THIS HAPPEN I NEED

DATE COMPLETED

WHERE

SOLO – WITH

THE STORY

THE BEST PART

WHAT I LEARNED FROM THIS

WOULD I DO IT AGAIN?

Manufactured by Amazon.ca
Acheson, AB